Four Days
Darkness to Light

Ann Bancroft

Four Days: Darkness to Light

ACKNOWLEDGEMENTS

My gratitude to Steve Gough, Unity UK, for all his help, encouragement and support, especially with the abridged audio version of Four Days.

My gratitude also to Lois Elsden, author, whose advice and encouragement has guided this book.

My special thanks to my beloved family for all their love and support.

© Copyright Ann Bancroft 2019

ISBN: 9781072643050

Four Days: Darkness to Light

CONTENTS

Foreword

Part One: Darkness
Chapters 1-6

An idyllic childhood did nothing to prevent me living with distressing and conflicting emotions that caused deep unease as I grew into adult life. Usually bad experiences in childhood are blamed. This is why my story is different.

Part Two: Enlightenment
Chapters 7-8

These chapters are an account of an event that brought me understanding in an extreme and unexpected way. It gave me the feeling of moving from darkness into light. It is with me to this day and directs how I interact with every situation in my life, bringing love, joy, peace and freedom from fear.

Part Three: Light
Chapters 9-10

I have tried to describe the days, weeks, months after the event, but there are never words that are adequate. I was exactly the same, my circumstances were exactly the same, yet everything was different. Life was easy, full of joy, I was in control.

Part Four: Knowledge
Chapters 11-16

The years since that experience have been exciting, a journey of knowledge. It has been a journey that, to this day, I never hear emphasised in formal religion, but it is and can be the same for every human being. We just need to become aware of it.

FOREWORD

We live our lives in two ways. We are the person we present to our family, our friends, our acquaintances. We are the person we live with inside ourselves, our inner lives in our thoughts and our feelings. This is where we experience the emotions dictated by events and circumstances. When life is going well, the happiness and feeling of wellbeing is accepted as normal. When we tussle with difficulties, disappointments, sadness that life brings our way, it is a different matter. We usually try to talk about our problems with a friend, with anyone who will listen, but, however close that person is, we can never share the actuality of how the problem is affecting us. What our listeners hear is coloured by their thoughts and feelings at the time and interpreted through their mood and previous experience. Sometimes their response, unintentionally, does more harm than good.

I have discovered God is the only one we can share this inner world with, the only one who will know and understand exactly what we are going through, know how to give us the help we need. We are taught that God knows our every thought, something I have no reason to doubt. But what if we don't believe in God?

Throughout my childhood and teenage years I had had only a nodding acquaintance with God, but as a late teenager I began to go to church regularly. A happy and secure childhood, all the love I had received from my parents, had done nothing to prevent the mixed-up person I had become in early adult life. The churchgoing neither helped me nor rescued me. I still had only a nodding acquaintance with God.

A fear of death dominated my life from my mid-teens. I told no one. I would lie in bed at night checking my heart was still beating. If it had stopped I wouldn't have known, but there was no logic to my fear. Over the years this fear gathered other fears causing me anxiety and difficulties on an increasing scale.

I have attempted to explain how my fears and anxieties became unmanageable. I have tried to describe an experience that brought me joy and happiness beyond my wildest imagination, an experience that filled my inner world and *'made all things possible'* in my life at that time.

A book called *Return from Tomorrow* came to my notice a few years ago. It was written by an American psychologist called George G Ritchie.

George Ritchie wrote of an after-death experience that profoundly changed his life. I doubt very much that he would have made the decision lightly knowing it would challenge the respect and credibility he had achieved. He was held in high esteem in his chosen profession. He was President of an Academy of General Practice, Chairman of a Department of Psychiatry, and also founder and president of a Universal Youth Corps.

I have no claim to fame. I'm just an everyday sort of person, but the experience I had almost fifty years ago changed me in exactly the way George Ritchie was changed.

Beyond my comprehension, at the time, and always wanting to write an account of what happened to me, George Ritchie's book has given me a sense of purpose and direction that I was previously unable to find. As he did, I write in the hope my account will be of help to anyone who might read it, anyone who has the muddled emotions and dreadful fear of death that I had.

Our actual experiences were different in the way they unfolded, but the lasting effect on both of us, so similar. How can I compare myself with someone who held positions of importance as George Ritchie did? For me there is only one answer. Whether the most important person in the land, in the world, the Pope or the man who sweeps our road, we are all equal in the sight of God. The differences come in the way we each respond to God – or happen to come across Him as I did. Given the opportunity, His response to each one of us is always the same – pure, unconditional Love. I discovered there is no condemnation, no punishment, only Love.

Four Days: Darkness to Light

*'Each friend represents a world in us,
a world possibly not born until they arrive
and it is by this meeting
that a new world is born.'*

From *The Diary of Anais Nin*

PART ONE: DARKNESS

CHAPTER ONE

Several years before the event I am going to describe, a new friend came into my life in a very ordinary way, but it could never be said it was an ordinary friendship. A young woman about my age, her husband and three young sons moved into a house nearby.

From the moment I first met her, even from the time I first noticed her, Joyce fascinated me. She was really beautiful. She radiated joy and happiness and had enthusiasm for life that I found infectious. I would see her chatting with other neighbours and almost feel the pleasure in their conversation. She was so full of energy. I don't think she ever walked at less than twice the speed of most people. I had never before met anyone like her. Her husband was an evangelist and was often away on preaching tours. Despite the weight of responsibility, with three small boys, and, by then, another baby on the way, she always appeared carefree and full of self-confidence.

Four Days: Darkness to Light

It was my mother who started to talk to Joyce. She loved children and would stop and chat with her whenever they met. Conversation was easy with three small boys and a baby to admire. Less outgoing than my mother, it took me a while longer, but I gradually became involved, and then Joyce and I would also stop and talk every time we met. Her oldest son was the same age as my daughter, and the newly arrived baby son the same age as my baby son to within a week. There was always plenty to talk about.

The fact her husband was an evangelist impressed me, but I had little understanding of what that meant at the time. Joyce would tell me in detail about his work. I would listen fascinated, but the significance of what he was doing escaped me. I never made comments, never asked questions. I had no idea what to ask! Theirs was a world that sounded so special, so important, so different from the world I lived in, I had no point of reference. I had heard of missionaries. We had missionaries visit the church I went to. They told us about their work. We had never been visited by an evangelist.

Four Days: Darkness to Light

Our conversations may have been about the very ordinary details of everyday life, but Joyce had a way of always bringing God into them. She would frequently refer to '*the Lord*' with such confidence it was as if He was there with us in person. There was no awkwardness or hesitation. I had never heard anyone refer to '*the Lord*' with such familiarity, such ease. Certainly no-one in church ever talked in that way, nor did anyone else I had ever known. If Jesus was ever mentioned beyond the context of church services, it was with slightly hushed, reverent tones and a tinge of embarrassment.

At the time, I accepted it was the way Joyce always talked, but, in hindsight, I think she might have been doing so, deliberately intending to catch my interest. This she achieved but sadly I was too scared and too in awe of her to ask the questions I can only assume she was hoping I would ask. Her remarks were met with interested silence. It was polite to be interested, but that was as far as it went.

'*The Lord*', however, did have a place in her life as natural to her as breathing. She would refer to any problems, big or small, with total conviction that the Lord had them in hand. Money was not plentiful, and I remember clearly the day she told me with great enthusiasm that the petticoat she badly needed had arrived in the morning's post. Whatever she needed, whatever the size of the need, she would tell me the Lord would deal with it. Of course, I knew the Lord dealt with bigger problems, like world peace and looking after the Royal Family. I had never experienced the suggestion in church services that God would be the slightest bit interested in petticoats.

But it was the way Joyce talked about death and dying that impressed me most. These were subjects I could hardly bear to think about let alone voice, yet she talked with a confidence that was incomprehensible to me. The subject dominated my unspoken thoughts. I told no one.

CHAPTER TWO

I was amazed Joyce was the slightest bit interested in befriending me. The differences between us couldn't have been greater. Self-confidence had never been my strong point and I was often bullied at school because I was an easy victim. One of my classmates once called me a weed. We were fifteen at the time. She shouted across the classroom. Everyone stopped chattering. Everyone heard her. I believed her. Whatever being a weed meant, I knew it must be something pretty bad. I was convinced no one would ever want to be my friend again.

The girl's mother had recently died and a short while after, the school nurse found she had nits. In those days, the treatment was to shave heads and she had to wear a woolly hat to school. She was angry with life, and I was the easy target. That had no meaning for me at the time and her remark did a lot of damage. It warms my heart now to remember how her hair grew back, thick, a beautiful colour and with lovely curls. She had the most beautiful hair in the class. Suddenly she was confident and popular again!

Spiteful remarks from a teacher did nothing to help. I was doing exactly the same as everyone else, but it was me she picked on. I guess even she sensed I was an easy target. If only teachers realised the power they have beyond teaching and discipline and what damage they can do to fragile minds. Later in life I was told to grow a second skin. What that meant or how to do it was not explained. There were positive remarks, but it took many years for me to remember them. Now, looking back, I realise I made life-long friends, and recall teachers who kept in touch for years after I left. Because I failed to recognise and give value to so many relationships, the pleasure and benefit they would have brought into my life was lost on me.

And so, I began adult life with low self-esteem and very little self-confidence. There was no explanation for this. Certainly I couldn't have been more loved, and despite the war years I couldn't have had a happier childhood, but feelings and emotions were not talked about then as they are now. It never occurred to me to go home and tell my parents what had been said. I have no doubt they would have listened but, generally speaking, children were left to fight their own battles.

I had had an almost God-free childhood. Neither of my parents felt the need for religion. I would guess things had been much the same in their childhood although I believe my mother and her sisters were sent to Sunday school. Often this was with the purpose of occupying the children and giving parents a rest.

However, church going, or Sunday school, was not part of my young life. When I started school there were Christian biased assemblies every morning, but I don't think I paid much attention. I can remember reading and rereading the school motto which was on a plaque on the hall wall. The message was *'A thing worth doing is worth doing well'*, but I don't think even that had much effect on me other than the value of distraction.

I was the only child of my father's second marriage. A widower, he already had a grown family when he and my mother married. My mother had never been married.

I have no reason to believe I was anything but a welcome addition to both their lives. Being an only child, I enjoyed all the love and attention I could have wished for. Of course, there were the ups and downs of family life through my childhood years, but none stand out in my memory as causing me deep unhappiness or distress of any kind. I was just four when the war started but I was never aware of the fear or anxiety my parents must have been going through. At that time, we were living in a big city.

CHAPTER THREE

My father died when I was nineteen. It was my first experience of death and it took me completely by surprise. Looking back, I realise I only knew him as a father not as a man. I can put together what I have been told and feel pride and respect for who he must have been. He had two years in school from the age of nine. This was when the Board Schools made school attendance compulsory. By the age of eleven, when he was allowed to leave school, he was both literate and numerate and had perfect copper plate hand writing. In a class of fifty or more it still makes me wonder how so much was achieved in so short a time.

He started work and the money he earned was given to his mother to supplement his father's poor wage. I am led to believe his father was a heavy drinker. The money my father earned had to be hidden in a tin in the garden and given to his mother as she needed it. Apart from the cheap sherry used in the Christmas trifle and a quarter bottle of whisky kept from year to year, there was never alcohol in the house. My father allowed himself two teaspoons of whisky in his first cup of tea on Christmas Day and the same on New Year's Day, which was his birthday! This amused both my mother and me but his resolve to avoid alcohol beyond that never wavered. I can only imagine what an effect his father's drinking must have had on him.

The memories I do have of my father are of a quiet, gentle man. He would sit in his big winged chair, puffing his pipe and reading or listening to the radio. He had the most beautiful, rich, baritone voice and would sing at the top of his voice every morning while he was shaving. Passers-by stood in the street outside to listen. I have wonderful memories of sitting on his knee, being cuddled, while he sang to me. I don't think he ever raised his voice or got angry with me. I cannot recall ever seeing him angry.

I was at a teacher training college and on school practice. I was already in the classroom ready to start the first lesson when I had the phone call. Mother just said, "Dad's not well. You should come home."

Four Days: Darkness to Light

It came as a shock. I knew my father was elderly, but his years meant nothing to me because he was so active. The family doctor constantly told us we would be sending him cards for his hundredth birthday and I believed the doctor.

Dad lived just three days after I got home, but it was enough time for him to tell me how wonderful my mother had been to him. She had carried the full weight of his illness alone. Innocent in such matters, I did not realise how difficult that must have been for her, but, somehow, they had managed to keep the progression of his illness from me. Neither of them would have wanted to distract me. I wrote to them every day. The phone call came the first day Dad hadn't asked to see my letter.

Mother was twenty years younger than my father. She had tremendous energy and vitality and a level of self-confidence I wish I had inherited. She had a great capacity for loving and whenever or wherever she saw a need, she was always ready to help.

Four Days: Darkness to Light

As a single woman in the early 1930's, she had moved into her own house, taking out a mortgage with one of her sisters as guarantor. I believe it was very rare for single women to be offered a mortgage or be accepted for such responsibility in those days.

A generation younger than my father she had also started work at an early age. She was thirteen when she was sent to live with a middle-aged couple. They had a small general store and she was to help with household duties. The couple had no children of their own and they took her into their hearts and were really kind to her. She was in regular touch with them to the end of their lives.

At fifteen she moved into *'gentleman's service'*. She quickly progressed from kitchen maid to cook and remained a cook until she bought her own house. Even then she went back to cover dinner parties and other special events for the family, such was her passion for cooking. Every meal she cooked, even on ordinary days, was special and delicious. She, too, surrounded me with love and I never felt anything but secure and wanted.

Discipline was left to my mother. I was expected to do as I was told. Her word was final. I was never sent to bed or denied privileges which seem to be the punishments used in most families whether effective or not. I can't imagine I always behaved perfectly but punishing me was not her way. I was just told I was doing wrong and to stop. Maybe there was something in her voice that gave me no option. With such a happy secure, childhood I still wonder at the person I had become as I approached adult life.

CHAPTER FOUR

We are all aware of the physical world we live in. We make changes without hesitation as ideas occur to us. We plan a new kitchen, a new bathroom, a new car, giving our undivided attention to every detail. But we also live in this inner world, the world of our thoughts and feelings. We seldom, if ever, give this world the same undivided attention, or consider it is possible to make changes. Of course, if it is a place of happiness and confidence, a place where we live comfortably with ourselves, there is no need for change, but this was not so for me. My lack of self-confidence became a bigger and bigger problem and I am sure was the basis for the maelstrom of emotions that gradually came to dominate my life. I never thought to question or reason through my feelings in the way I reasoned through my choice of new curtains or the new dress. I never thought to consider whether I could do anything to make this inner world a more comfortable place.

By the time I was in my late twenties I was married with two small children, I was, to all appearances, a normal, busy housewife, ticking all the boxes of life in the 1960's. No one, not even those closest to me, would have suspected the jungle of emotions and anxieties going around in my head.

When we married, my husband and I came to live with my mother. We had the blessing of the vicar and the family doctor, and so were reassured. When we talked to the vicar about wedding plans, he had agreed it was the right decision. Sharing our thoughts with the family doctor, he had also encouraged us, saying that of course we couldn't leave Mum. Unfortunately, the circumstances demanded wisdom, maturity and unselfishness. I had none of these qualities.

Mother's health was already beginning to cause problems. A major operation three months before we married was unsuccessful and even caused further problems. Within four or five years her health had deteriorated rapidly. By this time, we had our small daughter and baby son. I was fortunate not to need to go out to work, but working mothers were rare in those days anyway. Looking after my mother, as her needs increased, was just the most natural thing to do. No other option would have crossed my mind.

Our world became a world of endless hospital visits and treatments, none of which made any difference. Some caused further problems. She developed mild anxiety and depression. It was at the time when there was great excitement about electric shock treatment which had become the cure-all for everything. Mother was persuaded to accept a trial session. She came home unable to walk, but gradually managed to shuffle round the house using a walking frame. The reason for this was not considered and she was persuaded to go for a booster treatment. This time she lost the use of her arms and legs and, although the use of her arms came back, she ceased to be able to walk. Again, no consideration was given to the reason. I was given a hoist which made it possible for me to move her from bed to wheelchair each day.

Nothing had been done to help wheelchair pushers at that time, so outings were rare. Fortunately, the beach was at the end of our road, so I would pack a picnic on nice summer afternoons and Mother, the children and I would enjoy an afternoon on the sands.

As time went by, balancing my mother's needs with those of my husband and children became increasingly difficult. Daily, I set myself unattainable targets and went to bed each night full of guilt when I had fallen short of the person I wanted to be. Frustration, resentment, fear of not coping became part of the inner turmoil I was already living with every day. As usual I shared my feelings with no one and how I was feeling would have been obvious to no one. My actions were not the problem. I could manage those. One day I found myself saying to a friend, *"I can manage my actions, it's my thoughts I'm having problems with"*. She didn't ask me what I meant and I'm sure she had no idea what I was talking about. We didn't share problems like that in those days. I don't think I understood what I had said, but the time was to come when I would understand I had stumbled on a vital truth about life.

There was, by this time, a fear and dread beyond my guilt. My fear of death, always in my thoughts, had become focused on the prospect of my mother's death. I have difficulty choosing words that describe the magnitude of this fear. We were very close, and I couldn't imagine life without her. After my father's death, mother and I had grown closer and closer.

This was the mixed-up person I was when Joyce came into my life. Little wonder I found it incredible that anyone could speak as easily, and with such conviction about death, as she did, when the thought of it was dominating and devastating me in the way it was doing. My inner life had become unmanageable.

CHAPTER FIVE

Despite Joyce's constant references to God, I never gave thought to what *I* actually believed. I had no certainty that God even existed. I went along with what I had been told. God was a nice idea and if He did exist I was told He loved me, so I had nothing to worry about! There was no common ground between what Joyce believed and my perception of God.

As our friendship became closer and more relaxed, I developed a habit of continually telling Joyce about the problems I believed I was having, how unfair everything was especially as I was doing my best. I'm sure I was trying to convince myself that I was doing nothing wrong, that nothing was my fault, but it is not easy for the listener. One day, after allowing me to moan and complain for quite a while, Joyce simply said, "*I hand all my problems over to the Lord*". She had said this so often before. For the very first time I actually heard what she said, and the thought persisted.

Joyce had not explained how to hand problems over to God but later that day I went up to my bedroom. Alone and quiet and having no idea what I was doing, I collected all the problems into an imaginary bundle in my thoughts and handed them over to an imaginary God. It could only have been instinct that prompted me to do it in this way, but I was not aware of the power of instinct at that time.

What happened next took me completely by surprise.

I don't know what I expected if I expected anything at all. I certainly didn't expect what happened.

Suddenly – it happened suddenly - it was as if a great weight was lifted from me. It was as if all my problems had melted away in one instant. It was unimaginable, incredible. I am unable to find words to express the feeling of exhilaration and release that I experienced. All my worries, all my anxieties might never have existed. A feeling of total peace and well-being filled my thoughts.

Then I began to feel uneasy, insecure, uncomfortable, a stranger to myself. This wasn't me! This was far too easy. It couldn't be right!

Four Days: Darkness to Light

I quickly and deliberately made myself think of all the problems I had bundled up. I gathered them together in panic and forced them back into my thoughts. I gratefully found I was able to take back all the weight that had been lifted from me. Now, in what had strangely been my comfort zone, I returned to my daily routine. I went downstairs and got the evening meal. I knew who I was, and I was able to justify my existence again.

I told no one, not even Joyce. I had no understanding of what had happened.

To this day I wonder why it never occurred to me to tell Joyce, or to connect it to how I saw her living her life. Even more surprising was the fact that after years of churchgoing it should feel so wrong to feel so good.

I had often heard Matthew 11.28-30 (NIV) read in church services.
'Jesus said, learn from me and you will find rest for your souls, for my yoke is easy and my burden is light'.
It had meant nothing to me.

I had never heard anyone tell me how to understand and follow this advice or how it would make me feel if I did.

I guess psychologists would say God was not necessarily involved. Letting go of a problem is a technique they advocate anyway. I would agree, but as the suggestion came from Joyce, and, knowing her belief, I had been given reason and purpose. Sadly, I was not aware of and did not understand the magnitude of what she had shared with me. I'm not sure Joyce understood the magnitude either. She never questioned. She just accepted that giving her problems to Jesus to solve was the right thing to do.

As I have explained one aspect of life in my growing years was missing. My parents were not church goers. They were both of the opinion that it seemed to make little difference to the lives of those who went to church. I wasn't sent to Sunday school either, which was quite unusual in those days, even if parents had no interest in going to services. Mother insisted Sundays were family days.

Four Days: Darkness to Light

Through the summer months, we often went out to parks or on the bus to local hills where there was always a fun fair. Winter Sundays were made special because Mother lit a fire in the *'front room'*.

Those were cosy days. We would listen to the radio and make toast for tea on the open fire. Sometimes we toasted pikelets and ate them hot dripping with butter. My father would read his paper. Mother would write letters, knit or sew. This always surprised me. I was aware that it was generally accepted knitting or sewing, and horror of horrors, doing washing on Sundays was wrong. I was never sure why and never thought to ask. It was another world. It was a time of special closeness that I look back on with joy.

A family with three little girls came to live next door when I was five. The oldest was my age to within a few months and we quickly became friends. It is still a special friendship that has lasted for nearly eighty years. The three sister's lives were very much like mine except for Sundays. They all went to Sunday school. This made me consider them with childish awe.

One evening, we were playing together in the road outside our houses. A tall man in a long, black coat and black, brimmed hat stopped to speak to them. He smiled and chatted for a little while and then asked why they hadn't been to Sunday school the previous Sunday. I have no idea what they answered. I had gradually stepped back from the group.

Suddenly he turned to look at me. Unsmiling, he pointed his finger and said, '*Where do you go to Sunday school?*' Perhaps it was the blackness of his appearance, the coldness in his voice that made him appear ominous, but I was terrified. I mumbled the reason my mother always gave, that Sundays were family days. His response was to tell me, very firmly, that my mother was wrong and that I should go to Sunday school.

Without any experience of church going, this was my first encounter with someone who had chosen to represent God.

Maybe it was his threatening appearance. Maybe it was the stern, unsmiling face, but my first meeting with this man, who had decided his life's calling was to bring people to God, was not encouraging. I told my mother what had happened and asked if I could start going to Sunday school. Her response, as always, was to tell me once again that Sundays were family days. With no fear of divine retribution herself, she wouldn't have realised how I was feeling.

It took a long time for me to lose the fear that man created in me, but I would have been unable to explain why I felt such fear. Pastor of Hope Chapel on the High Road, he directed the lives of a small group of very dedicated *'believers'*. After that evening, whenever I had occasion to go past the chapel, I would hurry by as quickly as possible, never looking in the direction of the building. It always felt a dark, forbidding place to my childish mind. My friend has told me since that she had always felt the same.

CHAPTER SIX

As I got older God did creep into a corner of my life in a happier way. One of Mother's sisters was my godmother and she took this responsibility very seriously. She had been a nanny in *'gentleman's service'*. She had enjoyed a life style very different from that of her sisters. Living *'upstairs'* with the family, she had shared all the advantages and privileges denied her sisters whose time in service was spent *'below stairs'*. She was always considered to be the posh member of the family. She loved children but had never married. Consequently, I became a very special and much loved addition to her life and she was a very special person in mine.

She was a frequent visitor through my childhood years and took an active part in my growing up. She always came for my Christmas and birthday parties, something my mother managed to achieve throughout the war years. Mother would make little gifts for us all despite the difficulties. We would all have at least three small parcels off the tree at my Christmas parties. Preparing the party food was another challenge. Fortunately, my birthday was in June so she had six months to collect what ingredients she could find for each party. The tables always looked so inviting. She was especially good at making the most of what she had. She made jelly and custard look so different in so many dishes, we never realised that whatever our choice the ingredients were exactly the same!

My aunt would organise the games and they were always great fun. I think my favourite was when she gave each of us the end of a ball of string. We had to follow the string, which was twisted round furniture legs taking us into different rooms and round banisters, winding it into a ball as we went, until we reached the present at the other end. The string would take us upstairs, downstairs and back upstairs again. There was quiet concentration as we each tried to find the present. The love she brought into my life was and still is very special to me, but always in that love was serious intent.

A church goer herself, she constantly worried that I neither went to Sunday school nor was I taken to church. Despite all efforts to persuade her, Mother would not change her mind. I went to stay with my aunt sometimes, and on those occasions I was always taken to Sunday morning services. I dutifully sat through readings, prayers and sermons that didn't mean a thing to me, but my aunt was content. She was fulfilling the promise she had made at my christening. I was happy to please her, with the added bonus that it was my opportunity to *'do the right thing'*. There was such emphasis on doing the right thing in so many aspects of life, in those days.

When I was seventeen, we moved to live by the sea. Church going, or the lack of it, had come to weigh on my mind. I knew it would make my aunt happy if I started to go to church, but I suspect it was the pastor of long ago who had had more effect than I cared to admit. To this day I find it difficult to give him such credit. I feel sad for him now. He had probably never experienced the depth of love needed for his chosen path in life.

A new life, a new beginning I decided I would start looking for a church. With so little experience of churchgoing, I viewed churches with great apprehension. I wouldn't have used the word '*holy*' in those days but make use of the word now. I felt churches were such holy places that they weren't for me. Finding confidence to enter one on my own was not easy. Mother and Father had no objection to me going but were not inclined to join me.

I chose the nearest church to my new home. It took all my courage to walk into the building the first time. Finding a seat on the side aisle and near the back, I sat down, feeling I was well hidden behind a pillar. Unfortunately, I had chosen a '*paid seat*'. I was not aware there were such things as paid seats, but my knowledge of church protocol was limited. Perhaps there was a notice I didn't see, but I doubt I would have understood its meaning. I was to learn at a later date that it was church practice for members of the congregation to rent pews they particularly wanted. This made the pews available for their use whatever time they arrived for a service.

The people who had paid for the seat arrived. They were less than pleased to find me there and told me very sharply to move. Humiliated, I got up and literally ran out of the building. I kept my head down, looking neither right nor left, hoping I hadn't been seen by anyone else. It felt as if I had made a dreadful mistake and it weighed heavily.

However, I was determined to get things right in my new life and decided to try again. This time, at a different church, I was more successful. A lovely elderly gentleman, with a beaming smile and sparkling eyes, welcomed me. I met him in the High Street a few days later and he made a point of stopping to speak. He said how nice it was to have met me. There was no pressure or expectation that I should go to church again. There was no feeling of threat, as there had been with the tall dark figure so many years before. That lovely elderly gentleman, with his warmth and wisdom broke down many barriers for me that day. He was the loving face of God.

I began to go to services, but I would still creep in and sit behind a pillar, hoping not to be noticed. The vicar encouraged me to go to the youth breakfasts, held every Sunday morning, but I wasn't to be persuaded. I longed to go but couldn't face all the *'special'* young people who would be there. I was convinced they were part of a situation I wasn't special enough to belong to. I was still the *'weed'* I had been at school. I still lacked the simple confidence needed. I was so good at making excuses no one guessed the reason.

I continued to go to services with dogged determination and continued to sit behind a pillar where I thought I couldn't be seen. The service content meant nothing to me. I went through the ritual each week, gradually learning the words for each prayer and hymn, but they held no meaning for me. It was important for me to be there but for the wrong reason. I was just doing what I had been told was the right thing to do! Of course, I had been given no reason to think there was any more to it than that.

I must have given the impression I understood what it was all about, because the vicar agreed, without hesitation, that I should be confirmed. I always said so little that it had to be assumption on his part, but I'm ashamed to say my reason was not what it should have been. I wanted to be confirmed, because it was a condition for acceptance at the Church of England training college I wanted to attend. The college was only twenty miles from home making it easy to visit my mother and father. Being a church college meant I could continue doing what it was right to do, and its proximity meant I was still close to my parents. I had an answer to two problems at the same time!

I don't know what I expected from my confirmation experience, but I felt no different. My mother came with me. This made it feel a special occasion. The vicar gave me a little book in recognition of the event. I tried to read it many times, particularly the night of my father's funeral, but I found no comfort. The words were just words and were without meaning. The little book was called *My Faith*. It was obviously my faith that was missing, or maybe it was the dry, uninspired way it was written.

The Bible notes I had been told I should read every night had the same effect. Of course, I did as I was told. I struggled through the readings, night after night, dreading the effort but never questioning the fact I found the teachings meaningless. It was always such a relief when the nightly ritual was over.

Two years at the college of my choice, and a strong Christian emphasis on all aspects of college life, did nothing to change this. In my own defence, there was nothing to challenge me, to make me think it could be otherwise. I never seemed to hear about the joy and excitement of the Christian life in this world. Everything I did hear was about life hereafter with all its threat, or about protocol such as taking communion three times a year, and not having anything to eat or drink before going to early communion on Sunday mornings.

I went back to live with Mother after college, and resumed my church going. I always went home for holidays, and so had kept in touch with the church. Now I went with more confidence. The fact I had been at a Church of England training college seemed, in my sad way of thinking, to give me some credibility. It was the obvious place for my father's memorial service, and it was where I married two years later.

Four Days: Darkness to Light

My husband was a badminton player and very quickly joined the church badminton group. I explained to him that he should also go to the services on Sundays because I thought it wasn't right to take just the best things from church life. Such was my perception of church going! Fortunately, my husband came willingly and so, when the children came along, we went as a family. Mother began making cakes to support any events at the church and later came to services, even when she was confined to her wheel chair. The vicar, a lovely man, would drop in occasionally making us feel very cared about. It was strange but he always seemed to come when we were washing our hair!

Even with all this involvement in church life, I still went through the ritual in services with pious satisfaction. The words continued to have no depth or meaning. I wasn't looking for anything more, because I didn't know there was anything more. All I seemed to hear was what I needed to do for the church, giving, making cakes, supporting activities, going to services. It never occurred to me there was another side, a message that could change my life.

If I had been asked why I went to church I would have answered with confidence that it was the right thing to do. If I had been asked about faith I would have panicked. I guess I thought I had faith, but I would have had no confidence to explain what it meant. If I had ever given it consideration, I guess I had the thought there was a God, a God who loved me as long as I did the right thing.

Maybe there was also something in me that wanted to hide from believing. There was so much talk about missionaries. My history teacher left to become a missionary. Missionaries came to church services and talked about their experiences. I had a sneaking feeling that if I ever got too involved, I might be whisked off to deepest, darkest Africa or somewhere equally distant! Being the unadventurous soul that I was, this horrified me. If I stayed unnoticed, but still did the right thing by going to church perhaps I could avoid such an awful fate!

Quite by chance I happened to come across a radio programme that challenged my perception of God. It was a debate between two universities. The motion was, *'Is there a God?'*. The final vote was 15 against and 16 for. God managed to exist by one vote. I was astounded! I had expected absolute confirmation. I was sure these very clever, well educated people would know, would give me solid reassurance. I find it hard to believe now that I should have had such a strong reaction, but that night I felt like an orphan. There was probably no God after all. He was just a concept I was using as a crutch. That wasn't good enough. I felt totally bereft.

This was where I was when Joyce came into my life. I was confused, unsure, with no understanding of what having faith really meant.

PART TWO: ENLIGHTENMENT

CHAPTER SEVEN

As Mother's health deteriorated and she became confined to a wheel chair, she was totally dependent on my support. It was not possible for me to leave her for any length of time. This meant Joyce and I seldom had unrestricted time together. We would snatch a few minutes here and there, usually at my house.

Then one morning late in May, about three years into our friendship, we had a rare opportunity. Mother was away on holiday for a week with other people who had various disabilities. My husband was at work. Joyce's husband was on one of his preaching tours. The older children were at school and we had taken our small sons to playgroup. We eagerly settled down for a really good chat over coffee. We even had our favourite biscuits, chocolate digestives, bought as a rare treat in those days. Knowing we had the luxury of time for ourselves, with no other distractions, felt really special.

Four Days: Darkness to Light

I have no memory of how our conversation began. We had become close friends. There was always plenty to talk about. Suddenly the conversation changed. Perhaps Joyce made reference to something the Lord had done for her. That wasn't unusual and it was always without awkwardness or apparent intent to impress me. I had come to accept it as normal, but maybe for the first time I actually heard what she said.

I'm sure Joyce didn't expect the question I found myself asking. I didn't either.

I suddenly heard myself say, *"What have you got that I haven't got?"*

Where the question came from or why I hadn't asked it before, I have no idea. Even as I said the words, I wondered at myself. I wondered what I meant.

Joyce was Calvinist by belief, but that meant nothing to me at the time. She believed in heaven and hell and, without hesitation, had no difficulty explaining these facts to me in clear terms. I recall very little of what she said, in detail, but three statements stand out loud and clear in my mind.

- To begin with she said God was above all a judge.

She told me very firmly that God was not the easy-going God of Love held in popular belief by most people. I knew straight away I was one of those people! What I was hearing certainly turned upside down the belief I had, if indeed I had any identifiable belief at all.

- Then she told me that however good a life I lived in this world, it would be of no account in the next.

She explained that trying hard to do everything right, to live a good life would make no difference. This was more challenging information. I had never gone beyond feeling that if God existed and He was a God of Love, He would understand I had been doing my best. She said I had to do things God's way, not mine.

- She went on to talk about prayer and said that my prayers would rise no higher than the ceiling.

As prayer was not a part of my life, other than the formal prayers in church, this held little meaning for me. It was just something else I hadn't got right.

I think the conversation lasted the rest of our time together. I asked few questions. I held such respect for Joyce, anything she said had to be right. Our special time ended, and we needed to collect our young sons.

The day passed. I found myself pondering over our conversation. I said nothing to my husband when he came home. I doubt I would have discussed any details with my mother if she had been at home either.

That night was not a good one for me, but my husband and daughter were also restless. When they came down for breakfast, next morning, I discovered they were developing chicken pox. They both already had the first tell-tale spot. Our small son had just recovered but had obviously shared it with his father and sister. As the day progressed, they became very ill very quickly. The night was much worse than the previous one. We got very little if any sleep.

My mother returned from her holiday the following morning. She was exhausted and needing bed rest. Normally it would have been a case of responding to her physical needs and those of my husband and daughter, but I found I was distracted by a multitude of thoughts. In my mind I kept replaying the conversation I had had with Joyce. I was used to the turmoil already there but now all I could think of was finding a quiet place on my own. I needed to be alone, to find space to breathe, to consider what I had been told. Everything Joyce had explained was so opposite to my understanding of a probable God.

Finding space was impossible. With three invalids and a toddler to look after there was no opportunity.

I became more and more preoccupied but somehow managed to attend to their needs. Then my thoughts began to change. Now they were not specifically about my conversation with Joyce. I have no idea what prompted this change but very gradually I began to feel different, as if I had stepped outside myself. It was as if I was looking at myself as another person would see me. I became aware of all the problems and difficulties I thought I was having in my life in an objective rather than a subjective way. I began to understand how it would feel to be on the receiving end of me. I was not looking at the person I thought I was.

I was looking at someone who was self-righteous, resentful, frustrated, full of excuses, blaming everyone and everything else, taking no responsibility for my reactions.

I did not like the person I saw.

I began to realise that my reactions were entirely my own choice. I couldn't blame anyone else. However much I felt comforted by telling myself I was doing my best. I had no excuse.

The pain I felt became extreme and intense.

Four Days: Darkness to Light

Somehow, I got through the day. It was little different to the previous one. I was still being pulled in all directions. There was still no opportunity to have time on my own. Then a third bad night helped not at all.

The following day, my husband and daughter gradually became more comfortable as medication took effect. They went to bed early and settled to much needed sleep. Our small son had settled easily as he always did and Mother, also feeling better, was ready for bed.

At last I had time for myself.

CHAPTER EIGHT

It would be impossible to explain precisely what was going on in my head, but I revisited the thoughts I had been having during the day. In my arrogance I had thought I was doing pretty well despite my feelings of guilt. I had blamed everyone else for everything that was causing me problems, but had never looked at myself, at my responses, my reactions. My thoughts had changed direction. I was no longer feeling self-righteous about all I did, all I coped with. I was no longer feeling resentful because I wasn't appreciated. What I was thinking no longer had any direct connection whatsoever to my conversation with Joyce. This was not a choice I was aware of making.

Most difficult and most painful had been facing the problems I perceived were being caused by my mother. The closeness we had had and the love I had for her was being spoilt. It gradually began to dawn on me that none of this had anything to do with her. The turmoil in my thoughts was no-one's fault but my own. It was my self-righteousness, my self-pity, the way I responded to whatever was said or done that was causing the problems. Blaming Mother or anyone else was pointless.

I continued to realise that every aspect of my life was entirely my responsibility. I began to understand that every response to any situation or circumstance was my choice. In that moment the weight of these thoughts increased with intensity difficult to describe. There was no escape. I began to face what I was really like and the pain was intense.

Then I realised that if I had been so wrong about myself, I must also have been wrong about God.

The pain inside me became intolerable.

It was desperation that made me run to the little breakfast room at the back of the house. I fell to my knees, sobbing.

I said to God, even though I still wasn't sure He existed, *"I am so sorry I have misunderstood You"*.

It was all I said but it was said from the bottom of my heart. I had come to a place where to add one more weight to the weight I was already carrying was more than I could bear.

And this weight was the most dreadful of all. I had misunderstood God!

I felt myself letting go. I had tried so hard to do the right thing and achieved nothing. I began to lose awareness of my physical body where I was kneeling. Instead there came a sensation of falling. I was falling into darkness.

As I fell, it seemed as if everyone I loved was being taken away from me, rushing past me. I continued to fall deeper into the darkness and the darkness became deeper. It was as if I was leaving my husband, my children, my mother behind. I still fell.

My hopes, desires, frustrations and resentments and yes, my self-righteousness, followed as if they were actual things rather than emotions. They also rushed past me. There was nothing left except the darkness and silence. All I felt was emptiness. I have no idea how it could be but that was how it seemed. Strangely, I felt no fear.

Four Days: Darkness to Light

Then I began to sense I was not alone. There was someone in the room with me. My head was still bent and as I gradually opened my eyes, I could see the edge of a robe and sandaled feet. I found it impossible to raise my eyes higher because, as I tried, there was light so dazzling, so brilliant, I couldn't look up. I became aware the room was full of a light, so intense, it was beyond imagination, beyond description.

I make no apology for my explanation. Someone was standing in the corner of the small room, someone who was real, someone surrounded in and made of pure, brilliant, intense light. Light I could never have imagined.

I became aware of a feeling in my chest. It was a physical feeling. I can only liken it to air being blown into a balloon. At the same time, the brilliant light reached out to my body. It seemed to touch the depths of my being.

Suddenly everyone who had been taken away from me was being given back. It felt as if my husband, my children, and my mother were all back in my life again.

The light began to lose its intensity. Gradually I was able to raise my eyes. The figure in the corner, still clothed in light, began to fade, became transparent and was gone. I was alone in the room.

Feelings of pure ecstasy, joy beyond imagination swept over me. There is no way I can adequately describe the feeling. There are no words.

In that moment, I knew, beyond any shadow of doubt, death did not exist, does not exist. I knew it was a doorway we walk through. I knew with absolute certainty that we enter the next world exactly who we are but without our physical body. I was being told this was the same for **everyone**, again with absolute certainty. We read in John 10.9 that Jesus said, '*I am the gate'.*

In that moment, I knew, and also without a shadow of doubt that Joyce, as I had understood her, was wrong. How dare I think that! She was so charismatic, so sure of her faith, I had believed everything she had told me. It came as a shock. It was a shock hard to handle.

Four Days: Darkness to Light

As I knelt there, I realised all my fear of death had gone. The death I had spent so many years dreading, that turned me cold and petrified, did not exist. It really was only a gate to be passed through on the road through eternity. Life stretched endlessly ahead of me, but not just life, a life of joy beyond imagination.

Most important this was the same for everyone else too. It was beyond breath-taking. All the anxiety and fear about what would happen to those we love had been taken away.

C. S. Lewis, at the end of *The Last Battle* the final book in his *Chronicles of Narnia*, described how he saw death. He wrote, *'The term is over. The holidays have begun. The dream is ended. This is the morning. All their life in this world has been but the cover and the title page. Now, at last, they were beginning chapter one of the great story which no-one on earth has read and which goes on for ever. In which every chapter is better than the one before'*.

Every chapter is better than the one before – **for everyone!**

Four Days: Darkness to Light

I have no idea how long I stayed kneeling. I had no desire to move. I was in a place beyond my powers of description. I felt exquisite happiness, totally at peace with myself, filled with exquisite joy. Everything happy, wonderful, exciting, I had ever experienced, paled into insignificance. I didn't want to come back to this world.

Then, as if from a long way off, I heard an insistent voice saying my children needed me. Their actual names were used. I think it was the only thought that would have persuaded me to return to this world, but it was more than a thought. It was a voice that gave me the thought, a voice that made no sound.

I got slowly to my feet. I turned off all the lights and looked in on Mother who slept downstairs. She was fast asleep. I walked upstairs as if I was floating. I couldn't feel the treads under my feet that night.

My husband roused as I got into bed. I said to him, *"I've found what I have been looking for all my life and I didn't even know I was looking"*. Exhausted from three sleepless nights, I don't think he heard me. Then I slept, too.

The experience, I had just had, felt perfectly normal, the sort you could expect any night of the week! Years later I read somewhere God is NEVER sensational, but He is sometimes dramatic. What had happened was certainly dramatic. I had been given a new life, a new start, a feeling of a book of life where every page was wiped clean. I was totally changed but I was still totally me. How that could be I have no idea. All the spoilt and tattered pages of my life previously had been wiped away as if they had never been. I have no way of explaining what happened. It just felt normal. Maybe the normality was because I had been taken back to the person I was created to be. That normality, I had come to understand was the same for everyone.

I had been shown that The Light I had experienced transcends, in power, every form of material light. When we look to the source of that light great changes come about in our life and affairs.

PART THREE: LIGHT

CHAPTER NINE

Bright sunshine was streaming through gaps in the curtains when I woke next morning. The night had been good, unlike the previous three nights when the effects of chicken pox had given my husband, my daughter and me no rest.

In the instant I woke, the euphoria of the night before swept over me. I had no time to remember the previous evening before the sense of utter peace and wellbeing filled my consciousness again. It came as a surprise. I had had no thought for what to expect or even to expect anything from the experience. Then and only then I remembered.

I got up immediately and pulled back the curtains. I was not prepared for the scene before me. It was literally breath taking. The sky was a deep, intense blue, the grass a deep, vibrant green. The depth of colour was again beyond description and everything was more sharply and clearly defined than it had ever been before. I have no possible way of adequately describing what I was seeing but, like the night before, I felt no sense of surprise or disbelief, just pure pleasure. Sometimes I look again hoping to see the colours I saw that morning, but the depth and intensity are never there.

I have no memory of family members already awake except for my mother who was waiting patiently for my appearance. She was obviously better than she had been the previous day. I sometimes wonder what must have been in her thoughts when I went to her every morning. Facing each day had become something I dreaded. I never knew quite what I might have to cope with. The monotony and grind of routine took my energy and I am sure my weariness and lowness of spirit was obvious. All these years on, I realise how hard it must have been for my mother to be so vulnerable and so dependent on me.

I am sure she was confused when I went to her that Monday morning with a smile on my face that reached from ear to ear. I couldn't stop smiling. Every word I uttered felt so different. It was as if I was sharing the most incredible love.

Four Days: Darkness to Light

She made no comment that day, but she had noticed how I had changed. It was some time before she finally asked me what had happened. She said I was so different. Perhaps she had found confidence to believe her new daughter had really come to stay. I'm not sure what I told her, certainly enough to explain the change in me, but I found details impossible at that time. I was unable to find words that really explained what I was trying to share. Her reply was that she knew something big had happened. She didn't question what I told her, she seemed to understand.

Over the years, when we had had almost inevitable mother daughter differences, she would sometimes say, "If only you were different." I had always felt resentful. Wasn't I doing my best? I would feel outraged and self-righteous. I would try to justify myself by explaining my problems to anyone who would listen. Obviously, I was trying to reassure myself. Surely, I couldn't be the dreadful person that her comment implied.

Now, of course, I understand that what she said was never criticism. It was a longing to close the space between us that my reactions always created. I understand how unhappy she must have been trying to reach me, all that precious time wasted. She had been right. Now, despite myself, I was different. But, despite understanding what I had clumsily tried to explain to her, I don't think she could ever have imagined or expected the change that had taken place.

That first day stays in my memory in vivid detail. Circumstances were the same as the day before. I had two invalids recovering from chicken pox, a toddler and Mother needing the same amount of attention, yet the day was different in a spectacular way.

I had energy I had never before experienced. I would drag myself up and downstairs. Now I ran up and down effortlessly. Everything I did was effortless. Nothing was too much trouble. I rushed around… so much to do… but it didn't feel like rushing. There was positive enjoyment in everything I did, and I couldn't stop smiling. Mother must have watched in amazement. No one else seemed to notice. My husband and daughter were still preoccupied with chicken pox.

All the time I felt as if I had stepped over a wall and was seeing the world from God's side. It was how He meant it to be. Suddenly it was such an exciting, wonderful, beautiful world, and I was alive in it. Everything was exactly the same as it had been before, but it was also completely different. I was exactly the same as the night before and yet I was completely different. To this day I have no way of explaining this.

My godmother had given me a bookmarker when I was a child. It had writing on it. It said: '*Seek Me Early*'. I had no idea what it meant. If only I had understood. What a difference it would have made to my young life. But that is the problem. We don't realise, understand, or know, what a difference God makes until we find Him. As I said instinctively to my husband the night before, "*I've found what I've been looking for all my life and I didn't even know I was looking*".

CHAPTER TEN

I couldn't wait to see Joyce. We greeted each other as warmly as we always did. The smile on my face seemed to come from the depths of my being. It felt as if I was saying to her, *"Yes it happened!"*. She responded with the warmth she always did, but she didn't notice anything different about me.

This surprised and confused me. I expected her to know what would have happened, and to say so. I was sure it couldn't have been more obvious. I now look back in amazement at my naivety. I had assumed she only had to talk to anyone in the way she had talked to me, and what had happened to me would happen to them. I did try to say something, but the words wouldn't come.

Incredibly it was about a year before our coffee morning conversation was mentioned. I said very little and what I did say was again clumsily explained. Her response was not what I expected. She was annoyed that I had not told her before. She said she and her husband had been praying for me all through that year, and it had been wasted prayer time.

Four Days: Darkness to Light

With no understanding of the power of prayer or even how to pray, I also had no idea how much energy and determination it must have taken for them to pray for me for so long and with such dedication. I did not understand prayer as a practical tool for daily life. For me it was just a ritual you went through in church services. What I did discover was how deeply Joyce and her husband cared about others finding the joy they had found.

The smaller details of the week that followed have been lost in my memory, but I know without doubt that I woke every morning feeling the same as I did the first morning and every day was the same as the first. I coped with all I had to do with effortless joy. It was exciting and so different, but I just accepted how it was. It didn't occur to me to sit and think about the change in me with reason and logic.

However, there were three experiences that bore no relation to my daily routine.

Joyce's husband, as I have explained, was and still is an evangelist. He must have been at home that week because one morning I went to pick up the milk and happened to glance up the road to where they lived. Their car was parked outside the house. It stood out from all the others, because it was surrounded by a circle of light. I remember thinking that anyone travelling in the car would always travel safely, but what I was seeing strangely didn't surprise me.

I had a similar experience in the local bakery when I went to get bread. One of the assistants had an aura of light around her. She was serving customers, as were the other assistants, but she was the only one with the aura. Again, I felt no sense of surprise, it all seemed quite normal.

The third experience was of my own making. I was walking through the town centre one day when I saw a clergyman coming towards me. His dog collar gave him away. I positively beamed at him. Illogical as it seems now, I felt sure he would know what had happened to me and speak to me. I think I longed to connect with someone, anyone, who could communicate with me. I got no response. The poor man was obviously engrossed in his own concerns, maybe planning a difficult sermon. Anyway, I must have looked such an idiot and it is always best not to get involved with idiots. It could be so time consuming!

The change in me had happened on a Sunday evening, and had made me feel really excited at the thought of going to church. I longed for the next Sunday to come. Now I would belong. I would really understand what it was all about.

The day came and I sat in church waiting for the service to begin with great eagerness. It therefore came as a considerable shock to find nothing I heard connected to my new understanding. I was confused! When I knelt for the general confession, I remained quiet. I felt I had nothing to say.

After that Sunday morning, church going became a different experience for me. I continued to go to services with determination. Now I had confidence. It was no longer something I felt I should do, but something I wanted to do. I would listen intently to every word. The words were no longer lifeless and without meaning. They just didn't come to life in the way I expected. I kept searching for a connection. It was a long time before I was able to analyse and understand why. Eventually I came to believe that, for me, the structure of the services, the wording, was making God too small. Maybe we have needed to make God smaller than He is to be able to comprehend Him.

At home I was having difficulties, too. I had become Pollyanna overnight. I must have been very frustrating to live with. My thoughts were exploding with happiness. I wanted everyone to share that happiness. I found myself willing my mother, my husband and children to think in the same way, to feel what I was feeling. I couldn't bear to be in this wonderful place without them. I would constantly tell God that if my family couldn't have what I now had, then I didn't want it either. It didn't work like that. This was a choice I no longer had. It was not possible to go back to before as I had done on a previous occasion.

I craved harmony. I remember the children having a little squabble one lunch time. It caused me such distress. I insisted they *'make up'* immediately. I found I needed to replace discord with harmony as quickly as possible. I found that if a thought with a darker side crept into my mind, it was automatically pushed away. A happy, positive thought replaced it instinctively. This was not a reasoned response. I had made no deliberate effort to change the thought. It just happened.

With time, I gradually came to believe, and understand how important to our health, happiness and well-being our thoughts are. When I explained to a friend that I could manage my actions but not my thoughts, I unwittingly stumbled on a truth that was at the heart of the message Jesus had come to share, but even as early as Proverbs 23.7 we are told: *'As a man thinks in his heart so is he'*.

PART FOUR: KNOWLEDGE

CHAPTER ELEVEN

The weeks went by and turned into months and then years. It was like living in a bubble of peace and joy. Things did go wrong but they never seemed the disasters they had before and there was always a feeling that I could turn in thought to Jesus for comfort and reassurance. I had always had such a resistance to *'religious fanatics'*, yet here I was behaving like one and it felt quite normal, and quite wonderful.

From the beginning, I was conscious of being enfolded in a feeling of warmth. It was summer, the weather was warm anyway, but this warmth was different. It is again difficult to describe the reality of the feeling. It was a physical feeling, as if I had a soft, cosy blanket wrapped round me. I lived surrounded by that feeling of warmth for weeks, months, even years before it finally began to fade, or I became used to it.

The feeling that I had stepped over a wall and was looking at the world from God's side also persisted.

Four Days: Darkness to Light

The intense feeling of love was there all the time. Within that Love it was as if pieces of a giant jigsaw puzzle were falling into place.

It is not good to think or say *'if only'* but if only I had understood what had happened to me. If only I had been able to talk to someone who could have helped me understand the power I had been given. Now, all these years on, I believe it was the power Jesus told us would be possible when He went to His Father.

I hadn't confessed my sins. I suppose I had faced them, but I hadn't said sorry for them. I had said sorry to God for misunderstanding Him, but I had made no conscious decision to give my life to Jesus. God had just taken over and sorted me out, asking nothing of me. As someone said to me recently, *"God took you by the scruff of the neck"*. Obviously, He shook me into His reality.

The way my thoughts changed was dramatic and still amazes me. I have come to realise and understand the importance of our thoughts on a scale not easily or willingly recognised. Jesus spoke often about how we think. Passages are read as routine Bible readings in church but never really emphasised or given the vital significance needed. Our thoughts direct our lives. Mine certainly did and I had lived in a dark world for so many long years.

Now my thoughts were crystal clear. It was as if they had been washed in pure spring water or put in a strong solution of bleach and cleansed of all that had distressed me. I was given control of them. I would never have expected it would give me such a feeling of freedom. Every thought I had was positive although I would not have understood them in that way, at the time.

Positive thinking was never mentioned when I was growing up, but it has become popular jargon over recent years. *'Think positively'* we are told. Athletes say that is what they are going to do before a competition. Friends say it in normal conversation, but it is said without any serious understanding or conviction. It can make a difference, but if we look behind a positive thought and there is still a feeling of doubt behind that thought, the positive thought loses its power, and has only superficial effect. In circumstances that create fear or anxiety, a bigger issue, the positive thought has to come from a *feeling* of certainty, for it to be effective. I have found this feeling of certainty, for me, comes from the promises Jesus shared with us.

Joyce had a strong belief in the devil. Not knowing what had happened to me, although I don't think it would have made any difference, she would constantly tell me not to let the devil in. Like George Richie, whose book I mentioned earlier, I didn't want to think of the devil. He didn't either. My thoughts, like his, were too full of Jesus.

As time went on, with this constant reminder of the devil, some of my earlier thoughts and feelings began to return. Inevitably there was conflict between what I felt I now understood and what I was being asked to believe by those who I was convinced knew far more than I did. It was beginning to cause me distress again.

Every summer a Christian convention was held in a marquee in a local park. When a friend called to ask me if I was going, we started a conversation and I shared my confusion, but not in detail. I said something had happened to me that I didn't know how to handle. He told me he had had exactly the same problem and I should read *The Power of Positive Thinking* by Norman Vincent Peale (NVP). I had never heard of the book but quickly bought a copy.

He was right! I was so excited to discover someone had actually dared to write in the way NVP had written. For me it brought Christianity out of church and into daily life, in a real way. It reconnected me to my joy and peace. It was exactly what I needed to give me confidence to believe what I now knew anyway. I was back in my bubble of peace and joy.

Over the years other writers have come to my attention. J.B.Phillips, who translated the gospels into modern English; Lloyd Douglas, who wrote *The Robe and The Big Fisherman*; Marianne Williamson, who told about her *Return to Love*; and Anne S. White, whose son was wonderfully healed. Each book came into my hands at exactly the time I needed it. Previously I had only read what was given me by the church like the little book, *My*

Faith. I had struggled with it the night of my father's funeral. These writers have all shared their faith in a way I could understand, but I have never once, since that time, taken on another's thinking if it hasn't been in line with what I had been told. Buddha said, *"Believe nothing, no matter where you read it or who has said it, not even if I have said it, unless it agrees with your own reason and your own common sense"*.

CHAPTER TWELVE

I often say, *"I will think of you"*, instead of *"I will pray for you"*, when I have concern for someone, especially if the person doesn't go to church. It is an awesome thought but perhaps all our thoughts are prayers. This would explain the circumstances in our lives, whether those circumstances are good or bad. We are often told, *"If you don't want it don't think about it"*, but we fail to give this advice serious consideration.

I didn't realise what I was doing but I began to use prayer instinctively. My small son started complaining about a nightmare. He became distressed each evening at bedtime. I would sit on his bed and try to reassure him but nothing I said seemed to have any effect. One night I said to him, *"Shall we ask Jesus to take away your nasty dreams?"* He nodded. I put my arms round him and simply said, *"Jesus, please take away these dreams"*. There was no amen or any words that made a prayer, a prayer in the way I was used to, or any expectation of outcome but the nightmare was never mentioned again. No one was more surprised than me.

It was a long time before I really came to understand and use prayer effectively. I had no idea why we prayed or what purpose it had. Today, my first reaction in any situation is to pray. I have learned it is a practical tool for living, not the pious activity I had always experienced in church, where it had just seemed a routine requirement.

I am so much like Thomas who needed proof to believe. One day I read that research had been going on into the efficacy of prayer. Someone on one side of a building was told to pray positively for someone they didn't know who was on the other side of the building. The person being prayed for was monitored and there was a definite change in their well-being. Another person was told to send hateful thoughts to a person a distance away. The lowering of their well-being was measurable. Neither recipient knew this was happening.

I had never been aware of the promise Jesus made, but I pray now remembering that promise. Mark 11:24 tells us He said: *"Therefore I tell you whatever you ask for in prayer believe that you have received it and it will be yours".* This promise is repeated in all four gospels. It is an amazing promise that is seldom discussed. I find this difficult to understand. Recalling this promise makes me feel confident when I pray.

Of course, sometimes it feels as if a prayer hasn't been answered. I guess, *'If it be Thy will'* prayers became a way of explaining unanswered prayer, but Jesus didn't say God would consider what I pray for and decide whether or not to give it to me. He said we can have what we ask for. This opens up a problem, but only if we can't accept that maybe the answer lies within ourselves. How much faith did we feel when we prayed? How much dedication and determination did we have? Was it something we felt we ought to ask for, but didn't really want? We need to pray with the firm conviction that God has our best interests at heart. We need to be specific in our prayers. God is not trying to trip us up, give us second rate answers or make life difficult for us. We do that for ourselves.

I have discovered the way we pray is important. I have learned not to give God a shopping list and then keep repeating it as If He hasn't heard, as if I don't trust Him. If I plant bulbs and constantly dig them up to see if they are growing, they are unlikely to flourish and bloom. Not to keep repeating a prayer is very difficult, especially if it is about something causing considerable anxiety. But I have read about possible, practical solutions that give me real help. These ideas inevitably come from groups outside the established church.

I have taught myself to say *'Thank you God'* every time the problem I have prayed about comes to mind, knowing God's power is working on my request. I am always amazed at the peace and reassurance this gives me. I also thank God for His love and care for me. I thank Him for any other blessing big or small that comes to mind. It might be for the special and constant love I receive from my family, from my friends. It might be for my home, for a warm bed, for my food, or it might be for the lovely plumber who came immediately to deal with a small leak and then stayed to chat with me because he thought I might be lonely. It might be for the beautiful sunshine that makes the raindrops hanging on the washing line sparkle. My husband taught me to do that. He would say there is magic in everything if we look for it.

Thank you is so important. From the first day after that May evening, I found myself consumed with gratitude. I would walk round the house whispering thank you God time and time again. It was instinctive. I didn't need to remind myself. Over time I have found gratitude is a magnet that draws to us friends, love, peace, health, material good and answered prayers. When we are grateful for the blessings we already have, our gratitude attracts extra good. True gratitude is a spiritual quality that is built into the soul. It makes us aware of what we call blessings that would previously have gone unnoticed.

Every night before I go to sleep, I try to think of twenty things that have happened during the day that I can thank God for. It may be for answered prayer. It may be for a seat on the bus. It may be for the hug when I met a friend. It may be for bigger things like a wonderful family party. I find if I don't do this, I notice the difference. I have no idea why it has such a marked effect, but it does.

CHAPTER THIRTEEN

From the beginning, I found I had a desperate need to read the Bible. I would look for a way to escape, a way to be on my own, usually upstairs, even if only for a brief while. I would lie on my bed and open the Bible at random. I would read with what I can only describe as thirst. The words that had previously held no meaning seemed to rise from the page. Now I found in them an exciting depth of meaning. What a waste of time it had been to spend all those agonizing hours doing the right thing and struggling through Bible passages of dead, meaningless words.

I came to see the Bible as a handbook for life, and the author was God. Great responsibility rests on a Creator. He had made sure there was everything there to make our journey through this life a wonderful experience. Self-help books have become the norm on bookshop shelves today but, useful as they can be, the Bible has God's support system! Hearing passages read in church, in formal ways and by robed figures had, for me, distanced it from its purpose. Now it seemed a part of normal life, like a recipe book and my life was dependent on how carefully and willingly I followed the recipe.

My favourite Bible verse quickly became *'Perfect Love casts out all fear'* John 4:18. No longer did I lie awake at night with dark thoughts. Little fears disappeared as well as all the big ones, and without fear came so much understanding. I found myself knowing how Daniel had been able to spend time in the lion's den and survive, or how David was prepared to fight Goliath. They had had no fear. Random, unconnected events would come to mind. All made sense, became real in a way they never had before.

However, I gradually became aware of a wealth of reading beyond the Bible or anything I had heard about previously. As I have said, I was often led to exactly the right book at my point of need. These books, by authors I have mentioned earlier, always brought what I was reading in the Bible into the reality of modern life.

The Bible verses of particular interest were those describing physical healings. At the same time, I was told there is no death. I was also told I need never be ill again. To describe the impact of this thought is something else difficult to find words to describe. I was told *need not* rather than *would not*, but, so convinced of the reality of the thought, I knew I had to discover more. Jesus spent His ministry preaching, teaching and healing. He told us we would be able to do the same because of His power when He had returned to His Father, yet the healing aspect is almost entirely overlooked. I know healing is a broad term, but I am referring to healing of our physical bodies. Apart from occasional special services in some churches when a *'healer'* visits, it is not an obvious and integral part of church life. Anyone in the congregation who would like healing is often invited to go to the front for prayer after the service has finished. Services where healing is the main focus of power are rare.

I brought up the subject of healing in my own church. The vicar at that time was not pleased and I was soundly told off. Jesus healed with total confidence and gave thanks for the healing before it happened. On one reported occasion where nothing happened, He didn't give up and walk away, He tried a second time and a successful healing took place. I was confused, especially knowing what Jesus had told His followers.

I found I needed to look outside the church to find teachings that made sense and spoke to me of the reality I had found. I read about a young woman, who had only months to live. She had been told, as a child, she had inherited a weakness with her lungs. When the doctors diagnosed consumption, she believed them. Then she happened to hear a speaker who was visiting the town where she lived. He told her she was a child of God and therefore could not inherit sickness. She became convinced she was meant to have perfect health. She set aside a special time for prayer each day. Her prayers were always prayers of gratitude and very gradually her health improved until she was perfectly well and able to bring up her young family. Neighbours and friends became interested. It was the beginning of a prayer ministry that has helped thousands of people with prayer for over a hundred years. To this day someone is always there to pray with you day or night.

I believe it is fear that prevents emphasis on healing. If healing is prayed for and doesn't happen it is difficult. That was the reason the vicar gave me for his anger. The *'If it be Thy will'* prayers maybe an insurance against this but their very nature suggests we are ready to believe a loving Heavenly Father is quite happy to inflict or allow what might be the most awful suffering on the *'child'* He has created. There has to be a way of understanding otherwise Jesus would not have told us to preach, teach and *heal.*

Someone I met myself had experienced an amazing healing. A dear elderly lady allowed me to go and talk to her. She had been badly crippled with arthritis, her hands so twisted, doing anything was a challenge. Receiving healing prayer, at a special service, her fingers started to straighten. She told me she had been totally unaware of herself while it was happening. Suddenly amazement watching her fingers straighten made her aware of herself again. The healing stopped, but not before her fingers had become straight enough to be of use. She was convinced that her hands would have been completely healed if she had not become aware of herself. This has to imply that *'If we lose ourselves in God, so we find ourselves'*, as I did that night. Then our bodies or our emotions are healed.

Our daughter suddenly developed asthma. This caused my husband and me great concern, because my husband's childhood had been shadowed by severe asthma. I would sit in my daughter's bed at night. She would kneel on my lap put her head on my shoulder and sleep. It was a solution but not a good one for either of us. With the promise still so fresh in my mind that I need never be ill again, I also knew that this had to be the same for everyone.

Then a book came into my hands quite unexpectedly called *Healing Adventure* by Anne S White. It was, as I have said, something that often happened when I needed an answer. I only had to read the first chapter. She had a son who was a severe asthmatic. One night, kneeling by his bedside as he struggled to sleep, she came to the end of her own resources, the time when God speaks loudest. She heard a voice say, *"Give up your resentment"*. She thought long and hard about this. She realised she did hold resentment towards someone. She did exactly as she was told. Her son received instant healing. His breathing became normal and he did not have asthma again. I set about following the same advice. I realised I had allowed resentment to grow in my thoughts. I identified the cause and let it go. It worked. Our daughter did not have asthma again. This brings us back to the power of our thoughts.

My son, as a young teenager, had a bad stomach upset. He was lying on the settee, feeling very unwell. I sat nearby showing my concern. Suddenly I reached out and put my hand on his stomach in sympathy. He sat bolt upright! He said he felt perfectly well. The amazement on his face reflected mine. He got up and went off to pick up normality. I did the same. We didn't speak about it. I don't think I knew what to say. Ten years on from that May evening I still didn't understand.

Some churches or groups teach that illness is the work of the devil. This again seemed totally at odds with the understanding I had experienced. I find myself unable to believe in a devil as an entity. If indeed he exists, I feel very sorry for him. He is blamed for so much! Just as I had used God as a crutch without realising, I believe we use the devil as an excuse for not taking responsibility for our own wrongdoing. There is a verse in the Bible that says the devil disguises himself as an angel of light. I have failed to find an explanation that speaks to me. Anyone in the ministry I have asked has sounded as confused. Maybe it refers to a situation like one I found myself in. Someone in my life, who could have been described as an angel of light, caused discord. Her presence was resented, when her intentions were entirely good. She was doing nothing wrong, but the effect was difficult to handle.

CHAPTER FOURTEEN

It had been Joyce's way of talking about death that had made such an impression on me. It had been my greatest fear. Now I knew that what we called death was but the passing from this world into the next, leaving our physical body behind. Now I could talk like Joyce, with conviction.

The time came when my mother quietly and peacefully left this world in the early hours of another May morning. I knew for her it would bring release. There had been need for much nursing care and I remember a very strange sensation that first day. It was as if I no longer had need of my arms!

I have no idea how I would have coped if she had died in earlier years, but now I felt myself trusting her to God with peace in my heart. Of course, the parting was painful, and she left a huge space in our lives, but I was convinced that all was well for her. I was convinced that all the restrictions she had endured for so many years were over. I had to be glad for her in my sadness. None of these thoughts prepared me for what was to happen years later.

There are so many theories about what our souls might be like, but I have to believe we will still look ourselves when we have left our bodies. Twenty years after my mother's death something totally unexpected happened. Often, of course, I still thought about her, but she was no longer in my every waking thought. Then one morning I felt what I can only describe as a tap on my shoulder just as I was coming out of sleep. It would be something of an understatement to say I was surprised to '*see*' my mother.

She was surrounded in light. She looked absolutely radiant. I could never have imagined such radiance. Once again it is not possible to describe it adequately. I had never seen her, even in the days before her illness, even in the days when she was in perfect health, looking remotely like I saw her that morning. Incredulous, I found myself saying, *"Oh Mum, I've never seen you looking so well."* She responded by telling me she had brought my grandmother to see me. *"But I don't know my grandmother*", I said. To this she replied, "*I know, that's why I've brought her to see you*". My grandmother had died while I was still a baby, but I recognised her from photographs. She was sitting nearby together with one of mother's sisters. Then they faded from my sight, leaving me with a feeling of utter peace and joy.

Mother spoke to me in words I could hear but they had no sound. This suggests we communicate by thoughts in the next world and the thoughts are words that have sound there, as words do in this world. When I was told to come back because my children needed me, it was in words I could hear but they had no sound either.

My godmother died two years before my mother. She was no longer living with us but still living nearby. As her health deteriorated and she became unable to visit us, I would call round to spend a short while with her most evenings after the children were in bed and before I settled my mother for the night. She eventually had to go into hospital, but she was still near enough for me to call in to see her almost daily if only for a short time.

My last visit, the day before she died, was very special. When I arrived, she was sleeping, but sensed my presence and soon opened her eyes. She enquired about my mother, her sister, and the children. She said how lovely it was to see me. Then she suddenly looked past me and said, *"Who have you brought with you?"* I knew there was only a wall behind me, and my instinct was to say, 'No one'. Instead something made me ask, *"Who do you think it is?"*. *"Why it's Stanley and he's praying for me"*, she replied. Stanley was a much-loved brother-in-law, who had died many years earlier.

I longed to stay with her but that was impossible because of my mother's needs. However, I came away feeling all those she had loved and who loved her were near her, waiting to welcome her. Next morning, the phone rang early. I was able to receive the phone call, telling me she had died in the night, with a feeling of peace.

I am sure many psychoanalysts would do their best to explain these two events in a very different way to the way I know they happened. Maybe they would suggest they were figments of my imagination. But I could not have imagined Mother's radiance. It was literally beyond my imagination.

J.B.Phillips, who translated the gospels into modern English, had similar experiences. He wrote in his book, *Ring of Truth* that he was sitting one evening when C.S.Lewis, who had died several days before, '*appeared*' sitting in a chair a few feet away from him. He spoke a few words that were helpful to difficult circumstances J.B.Phillips was going through. He appeared again a week later and repeated the same message which was very important to J.B.Phillips, who described him the first time as '*positively glowing with health*', and the second time as '*even more rosily radiant than before*'. J.B.Phillips had not been thinking about C.S.Lewis, whom he had only met once. I had not been thinking about my mother.

The church has a tendency to hide these experiences. Sadly J.B.Phillips was uncomfortable about what had happened with C.S.Lewis. He eventually shared the details with a kindly bishop, who put an arm round his shoulders and said, *"These things are happening all the time"*. What a pity they are not openly acknowledged. We ought to be able to talk about them with ease. I believe they would make such a difference to the life and vibrancy of our lives. They might take away so much fear and put dying into perspective.

Sadly, in the early days, I was told by a *'born again'* Christian that because Mother had not been *'born again'* she would go to hell. It is beyond me why this had been assumed. It is beyond me why it distressed me as it did. It certainly didn't fit with the understanding I had been given. Mother was one of the only two people who had recognised and understood the change in me. She had accepted and believed what I had told her without question. She didn't however, like me, talk in saved language. She didn't talk about being *'saved'* and giving her life to Jesus. She lived her faith, but, because she didn't fit the mould, she was judged by those who had no power to judge.

It so happened she was not well that night and I stayed with her. I didn't sleep. I found my thoughts wouldn't let go of what I had been told. Why I accepted and even thought about such comments, despite what I knew, is beyond my comprehension even all these years later. I found myself telling God repeatedly that I forgave Mother everything – not that she needed my forgiveness. I had had the most loving and caring of mothers. I was the one who needed her forgiveness.

Next morning, opening my Bible at random, the sentence, *'Whosoever you forgive, I will forgive also'*, leapt from the page. It was as if the words were written in gold. From that day to this, I have no memory whatsoever of anything I ever imagined Mother had done wrong. I use *'imagined'* deliberately. I would like to believe she has forgiven her spikey, often difficult daughter for things I did wrong. Never, since that time, have I been tempted to listen to anyone who tries to share fear instead of love.

CHAPTER FIFTEEN

As I had changed, my relationships changed. One relationship changed in a spectacular way. I never got on particularly well with my sister-in-law. I always felt threatened because of her, but not by her. Beautiful, athletic and confident, she was all the things I wasn't. The first time I saw her after that eventful evening we were suddenly close and quite at ease with each other. I felt bewildered but said nothing. I felt she had changed but maybe it was only the change in me that made it feel like that. We became the closest of friends and her early death left a huge space in my life.

George Ritchie had the same experience with his stepmother. All the resistance he had felt towards her disappeared and a caring, understanding relationship developed. He had the opportunity to explain the change to his stepmother. Sadly, I didn't get that opportunity. Mary had started to ask questions about what I believed. We had arranged an evening together, but her sudden and unexpected death came first.

All my friendships changed but it didn't feel as if it was anything to do with me. Perhaps everyone began to feel more comfortable with me because I was now comfortable with myself. It is the only explanation I can think of. I discovered I no longer worried about what people thought of me or about me. I found I could admit when I was wrong without it causing me pain or resentment. I could say sorry without feeling diminished. I was able to see the other person's perspective on a problem. It sounds so simple, but it brought such a feeling of freedom in all my relationships.

I also felt an overwhelming sense of oneness at the heart of all relationships. I felt an overwhelming sense of oneness at the heart of all religions. Absolute conviction dawned on me that there are no dividing lines in God's eyes. The dividing lines are misinterpretations of truth. The differences, the discord, the self-righteousness, all come from the mind of man. The rules for this and restrictions for that make the simple truth complicated. It becomes hardly recognisable. What a long way we are from the simplicity of the hillside meetings where Jesus shared God with us. We are all children of God. We have all been created in His image, so we are all equal and equally loved in God's eyes. What we do with, and how we respond to, that Love is our choice. *'God's gift to us is life. Our gift to God is how we live our lives.'*

When I was first confirmed into the Church of England, when I was seventeen, I was told I must take communion at least three times a year. Dates were specified. I was also told I must have nothing to eat or drink before I went to 8 am communion. Times have changed now but the way Lent is approached by the church hasn't altered over the centuries. It mystifies me. The churches become sombre places. There are no flowers, and purple is the preferred colour for altar cloths. Members of the congregation plan what they will give up for Lent. I have no difficulty accepting this, but why is it assumed Jesus had a difficult time in the wilderness? This doesn't make sense to me.

I believe the time was, for Jesus, a time of exquisite joy. I feel it should be a time of joy and celebration and maybe reflection for His church. He had just received all the power in the universe, but He needed time and space for the realisation of who He was to become part of Him. He needed time to understand the power that was now His. Why do we suppose He had a problem with the devil? He could heal, walk on water and change the weather. He just needed to be alone to think, to consider the knowledge, the understanding that was now His. Perhaps making special effort to do positive things for ourselves, for our community, for the needs around us should be the intention during those forty days, rather than *'giving up'*.

CHAPTER SIXTEEN

So, after all the years where am I now? What do I truly believe? I believe our time spent in this world could be the most wonderful adventure. It could be the most exciting adventure. I believe we are meant to have perfect health. I believe there is a God-shaped space inside each one of us and it is only when we connect with God in that space that we are able to receive fully the wonders He has prepared for us. I believe God has no favourites.

I believe God never holds back what He wants to give us. I believe He takes every opportunity to help us connect with Him. I was fifteen, sitting in an English class. The heat was stifling making it difficult to concentrate. The windows were open but that made little difference. The English teacher was introducing Wordsworth's Intimations on Immortality. Suddenly I heard the line, *'Trailing clouds of glory do we come from God who is our home'*. Wonderful imagery came into my mind making me forget all my discomfort. The teacher continued to read but I heard no more. I did not consider why it held such depth of meaning for me at the time, but I do believe it was God's first attempt to tell me who I am.

The poem goes on to say *'Shades of the prison house begin to close around the growing boy'* – and presumably girl too. The experience I had that May evening wiped away the shades of my prison house. It was like stepping out of darkness into light. It changed me on the inside and my perception of just about everyone and everything on the outside. Because I was vulnerable at that moment it was God's opportunity to confirm who I really am, who we all really are.

For longer than I can remember, I continued to wake each morning feeling exactly the same as I had that first morning. Every morning I was amazed by the utter joy and peace. It was hard to contain my joy. I wanted to shout it from the roof tops, but always there was a small voice of reason in my mind that held me back from doing anything that would bring doubt to my sanity. I instinctively knew no one would understand.

I have never been able to easily call myself a Christian. The responsibility is enormous. I believe, without question, that Jesus was God. Jesus was not just a good man, or another prophet. I believe He was like a window that had the purest, cleanest, crystal clear glass which God's Love, Light and Power shone through without restriction and in utter perfection. Jesus had no ego to get in the way.

Early in my life I used to wonder how God could be in heaven and for it to be claimed that Jesus was God at the same time. Now I understood. If I call myself a Christian, and then fail miserably, I may be getting in the way of someone else's search for Him as so many did for me. I would rather be doing my best, as one of the crowd, sharing what I know and believe without hesitation when there are opportunities.

Lloyd Douglas used his novels to express his beliefs. In one of his novels – *Invitation to Live* – he wrote, *'There is no end to the obligation resting on a Creator'*. I believe God is responsible for us, just as we are responsible for our children. I didn't ask to be created and they didn't ask to be born. God's love is unconditional, as mine must be for my children. George Ritchie witnessed and experienced this unconditional love just as I did. But there is a condition. It requires more than knowing. It requires a response from us if it is to change our lives and enrich our journeys through this world. An electric fire has all the potential for heat, but until I plug it in to the power source, I don't feel the benefit. That doesn't mean God isn't trying to bring good into our lives all the time, but until we recognise that we don't feel the same benefit.

There was so much I believed God was telling me in those early days. I would be standing at the sink peeling potatoes and it was as if I was holding a conversation with the Being who was with me that night. It was a long time before I had the confidence to acknowledge, even to myself, that the Being, made of pure light, was Jesus. How dare I believe! Everything in me longed for confidence to allow myself to believe, but George Ritchie, wrote in his book, *Back from Tomorrow* that he had the same difficulty after his out of body experience. However, I think he did have the confidence to acknowledge the possibility more quickly than I dared.

Life became an exciting adventure. Each time I queried something in my thoughts the answer came immediately and made absolute sense in the light of my understanding. Of course, nothing was new. Multitudes before me had been open to the same understanding. Realities or possibilities were sometimes almost too incredible for me to dare to believe. Some were difficult to accept and believe because they were so opposite to what I had been led to understand, yet they all fitted perfectly into the bigger jigsaw of life I mentioned earlier.

One day, walking back from town, it suddenly came to me with clear conviction that heaven and hell are not places in the next world, they are states of being. I suddenly knew I could be in hell or heaven in this world in exactly the same way as in my future existence. There is no difference. The perfection of God's love, the perfection of His forgiveness would make a place of eternal punishment impossible. People are converted to Christianity by the fear of hell. I wasn't frightened of hell. The thought never crossed my mind. I thought I had got my idea of God wrong and I guess, being me, I would have accepted my punishment. But wouldn't it be absolute perfection if we are converted by the sheer power and wonder of God's love? Love changes lives. Love, not fear, can change the world.

I believe we need to know ourselves as we really are, not as we think we are, if we are to find this peace that passes all understanding. George Ritchie had to go on that journey before Jesus came to him. I had those four days of turmoil. It is a painful journey, but there is no condemnation from God while it is happening. He is just waiting to step in at the right moment. Truly facing oneself is perhaps the most painful thing we can do, but the freedom it brings is breath taking. The peace that passes all understanding really is beyond understanding. It is unimaginable and impossible to explain in words.

I read recently that our stories are not simply our own. They are part of the state of universal consciousness that Jesus called the Kingdom of

Heaven. I know now we can experience the Kingdom of Heaven while we are here on earth.

Ecclesiastes 3.12 says *'I know that there is nothing better for them than to be happy and enjoy themselves as long as they live'*.

It took Jesus and His sacrifice of love on the cross to make us understand. I believe we need to honour His sacrifice, not just by Good Friday and Easter Sunday services but by standing with Him, by sharing His overwhelming love for us all in every way we can. In His overwhelming love we can experience the Kingdom of Heaven while we are here on earth. In His overwhelming love there is no darkness, no condemnation. In His overwhelming love we can be happy and enjoy ourselves as long as we live.

EPILOGUE

I began with Joyce so I must end with her. We had very different journeys into faith, but the destination was the same. We had a rich rewarding and very special friendship over more than forty years, until for her, in the words of C.S.Lewis, *'The term was over and the holidays had begun'*.

I am eternally grateful to her for the way she challenged my thinking, for her dedication sharing her faith, and for the joy and delight in her friendship. Of course, there was a third Person in that friendship. How could it be other than rich, rewarding and very special?

REFERENCES

Back from Tomorrow
by George G. Richie

At the age of twenty George Richie died in an army hospital. Nine minutes later he returned to life. What happened in those nine minutes changed his life for ever.

The Power of Positive Thinking
by Norman Vincent Peale

Norman Vincent Peale combines the deep strength of his Christian faith with an understanding of psychiatry. He illustrates how faith and optimism and how an attitude of mind can change lives.

Return to Love
by Marianne Williamson

Marianne Williamson explains how using a loving approach in everyday matters can be the answer to problems in our relationships, our careers and with our health, making sure our lives are more peaceful loving and forgiving.

**Ring of Truth
by J.B. Phillips**

J.B. Phillips translated the Greek of the New Testament into modern English. He called it his testimony to the history and reliability of the New Testament. It tells of one of the most amazing accounts of life after death ever written.

**Healing Adventure
by Anne S. White**

Anne White became convinced that God's will for His people is wholeness in spirit soul and body. She developed an amazing healing ministry.

**The Big Fisherman (and other novels)
by Lloyd Douglas**

Lloyd Douglas was a minister in America. He wrote novels with a distinctly religious tone. He brought people, alive at the time of Jesus, into real life using bible stories and biblical text.

Four Days: Darkness to Light

An abridged audio version of
Four Days: Darkness to Light
can be ordered from:

Unity
10 Lake End Court
Taplow Road
Taplow
SL6 0JQ

Or online from www.unityuk.org

Printed in Great Britain
by Amazon